CRABS

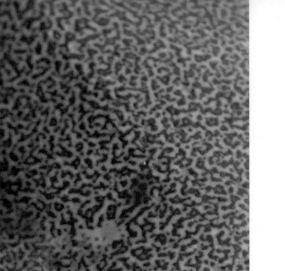

LIVING WILD

Published by Creative Education and Creative Paperbacks
P.O. Box 227, Mankato, Minnesota 56002
Creative Education and Creative Paperbacks are imprints of The Creative Company
www.thecreativecompany.us

Design and production by Mary Herrmann
Art direction by Rita Marshall
Printed in Malaysia

Photographs by Alamy (AF archive, FLPA, Amar and Isabelle Guillen–Guillen Photo LLC, K & P Photos), Corbis (Ingo Arndt/Minden Pictures, Ingo Arndt/Nature Picture Library, Jason Isley–Scubazoo/Science Faction, Scubazoo/SuperStock, Konrad Wothe/Minden Pictures), Creative Commons Wikimedia (Creative Commons Wikimedia, Dragon187, gargoylesoftware, Nick Hobgood, Jessica87nz, Wendy Kaveney, Stemonitis, Utagawa Kuniyoshi, Wilfredor, Doug Wilson, H. Zell), Dreamstime (John Anderson, Fiona Ayerst, Michele Cornelius, Alexandre Fagundes De Fagundes, Song Heming), Shutterstock (apiguide, Chabaphoto, C.K.Ma, Edgewater Media, eye-blink, feathercollector, Freer, Shane Gross, Botond Horvath, Jung Hsuan, indigolotos, IrinaK, Jonathan Lingel, macspike, marco, noppharat, fluke samed, Jeff Skopin, Beverly Speed, Teguh Tirtaputra, Hans Van Camp, Andre Valadao, Katherine Welles, wizdata, Michael Zysman)

Library of Congress Cataloging-in-Publication Data
Gish, Melissa.
Crabs / Melissa Gish.
p. cm. — (Living wild)
Includes bibliographical references and index.
Summary: A look at crabs, including their habitats, physical characteristics such as their chelipeds, behaviors, relationships with humans, and their threatened status in the world today.
ISBN 978-1-60818-565-8 (hardcover)
ISBN 978-1-62832-166-1 (pbk)
1. Crabs—Juvenile literature. I. Title.

QL444.M33G57 2015
595.3'86—dc23   2014028008

CCSS: RI.5.1, 2, 3, 8; RST.6-8.1, 2, 5, 6, 8; RH.6-8.3, 4, 5, 6, 7, 8

First Edition HC 9 8 7 6 5 4 3 2 1
First Edition PBK 9 8 7 6 5 4 3 2 1

CREATIVE EDUCATION • CREATIVE PAPERBACKS

CRABS

Melissa Gish

November marks the beginning of the wet season on Christmas Island. The first drops of rain trigger an

explosion of activity, as more than a million red
crabs emerge from the shelter of their forest habitat.

In the Indian Ocean, November marks the beginning of the wet season on Christmas Island. The first drops of rain trigger an explosion of activity, as more than a million red crabs emerge from the shelter of their forest habitat. Driven to mate, the crabs begin a perilous journey over open land to reach the sea. Cautiously, they climb down jagged cliffs to the rocky shore far below. The males travel first, each fighting to establish his own burrow. The females follow to mate with the males. The fertilized eggs hatch the moment they hit the water, and the tiny hatchlings float in the sea for several weeks. Millions of baby crabs then undertake the more challenging journey back up the cliffs and over dangerous ground to reach the safety of the forest, where they will continue the life cycle of the Christmas Island red crabs.

WHERE IN THE WORLD THEY LIVE

■ **Dungeness Crab**
Pacific coast of
North America

Atlantic Blue Crab
western Atlantic
Ocean and Gulf of
Mexico

**Christmas Island
Red Crab**
Australia's
Christmas Island

Snow Crab
northwestern
Atlantic Ocean
and northern
Pacific Ocean

■ **Japanese Blue
Crab**
Asian and
Australian coasts

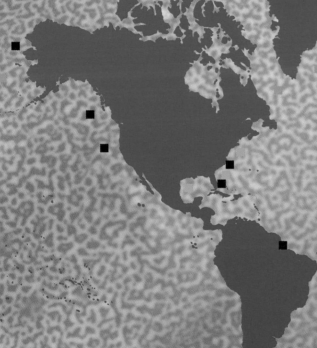

■ **Japanese Spider
Crab**
Pacific Ocean
near Japan

Mud Crab
estuaries and
marshes of Africa,
Asia, and Australia

■ **Fiddler Crab**
marshes and
beaches of
western Atlantic
Ocean

Approximately 6,700 species of decapod crustaceans
are classified as true crabs. While all crabs travel to water
to spawn, they spend varying degrees of their time on
land. Some species live in marine and freshwater habitats
around the world, whether along streams or coasts or
deep in the ocean. Other species inhabit forests, caves,
or beaches. The colored squares represent some of the
areas in which eight crab species are found today.

CRUSTY CRABS

Crabs belong to a vast group of animals called invertebrates, or animals that lack backbones (and usually other bones as well). Earth is home to more than 67,000 invertebrates classified as crustaceans. These are animals with branching, muscular limbs and a soft body protected by a hard outer shell called an exoskeleton. Some crustaceans are decapods, a word that comes from the Latin word for "ten" (*deca*) and the Greek word for "foot" (*pod*). The term refers to the number of **appendages** that these animals have. The roughly 15,000 decapod species include lobsters, crayfish, shrimp, horseshoe crabs, and crablike creatures—such as king crabs and hermit crabs—called anomurans. Only about 6,700 decapods are true crabs. These animals vary greatly in size. The smallest crab, named the pea crab for its size, survives as a **parasite** inside oysters, clams, and other shelled animals. The Japanese spider crab typically reaches 12 feet (3.7 m) across, from the tip of one leg to the tip of the opposite leg, and weighs more than 40 pounds (18.1 kg). It is not only the largest crab but also the largest crustacean in the world.

Female pea crabs grow to 0.5 inch (1.3 cm) in length, but males grow to only half that size.

Research suggests that crabs communicate through drumming their claws on the ground or by snapping them together.

The cyrique, a popular food on its native West Indian islands, tries to hide beneath rocks and plants.

Although all crabs begin their lives in water, they are highly **adaptable** and can be found in a variety of habitats. Snow crabs survive in the frigid Arctic sea, while the flamed box crab thrives in the shallow, sunlit waters of the Caribbean. In the Atlantic and Pacific oceans, living as deep as 4.3 miles (6.9 km) beneath the surface, 14 different species of vent crab live in communities where superheated water and gases spew from cracks in the seabed. About 1,300 crab species live in fresh water. The cyrique inhabits freshwater ponds and streams on Saint Lucia, Martinique, and other islands in the West Indies. Though abundant on some islands, the cyrique suffers from habitat destruction on Dominica, where the government established protected land to conserve it.

Many crabs live on land as well. The black-and-orange Halloween crab thrives in leaf litter in coastal forests from Mexico to Peru, and the blue land crab, found along the Atlantic coast of Brazil and in the Bahamas, hides in shallow burrows during the day and emerges after dark to hunt and forage for fruit, **carrion**, and live prey. Studies on blue land crabs have revealed that, despite being nocturnal, or active at night, these crabs will emerge from their burrows during

The nocturnal Halloween crab goes by several nicknames, including mouthless crab and harlequin land crab.

Coral crabs seeking protection
from predators benefit their
hiding places by keeping the
coral reefs clean.

the day to investigate the sound of fruit hitting the ground. Some crabs never see daylight at all, though. Nearly a dozen species of crabs in the Americas and on surrounding islands are characterized as troglobitic, meaning they spend their entire lives in the dark parts of caverns and caves.

Like all crustaceans, crabs are ectothermic animals, meaning that their bodies depend on external sources of heat, and their body temperatures change with the environment. Crabs do not expend energy to warm themselves, and most species have naturally low body temperatures. A crab's three body parts—the head, thorax, and abdomen—as well as its appendages are covered with a hard armor made of several **minerals** and a substance called chitin (*KY-tin*). The covering of the closely joined head and thorax is called the carapace. The small abdomen, which is tucked under the crab's body, is called the apron. Males have an inverted T-shaped apron, while mature females' aprons are rounder.

Crabs have five pairs of legs. The first pair is the largest. Called chelipeds, these sharp claws are used for feeding and defense. The males of most species have larger chelipeds than females. The next three pairs are pointed and are used

A flat body shape makes crabs well-suited to life in tight spaces such as rock crevices and reefs.

The red-spotted guard crab nibbles on corals but also protects them from more damaging predators.

After a crab molts and leaves its carapace behind, the excess water in its body turns into protein, helping it grow.

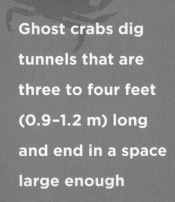

Ghost crabs dig tunnels that are three to four feet (0.9–1.2 m) long and end in a space large enough for the crab to turn around.

for walking. The leg joints have limited movement, so crabs walk sideways to keep from tangling their legs and tripping. Lastly, small, flat swimming legs are used like paddles in water. For land crabs, they may provide balance while walking. Crabs do not have lungs. Rather, they have pairs of gills that filter oxygen and send it throughout the crab's body. A crab must keep its gills moist, even on land. Most species have nine pairs of gills.

Unlike skin, which expands as an animal grows, the crab's outer covering stays the same size. As a crab grows, it must shed its exoskeleton so that a new, larger one can take its place. This process is called molting. Before it molts, a crab fills its body with water, swelling up and causing its exoskeleton to crack along a seam that runs around its body. Its back shell opens like a lid, and the crab pushes and pulls for about 15 minutes, dragging its appendages and body out of the exoskeleton. It leaves some body parts behind, including its stomach lining and a small portion of its intestine. Over the next several weeks, a new exoskeleton develops. At first, this exoskeleton is paper-thin, making the crab vulnerable to predators. For this reason, crabs tend to hide until

molting is complete. Most crabs molt 15 to 20 times in their lifetime.

Crabs have powerful vision. They can see movement all around, above, and behind them without turning their bodies. This is possible because their two compound eyes are situated on the tips of stalks that protrude from the head. Compound eyes are made up of hundreds of tiny cells, each covered by an individual lens. Some cells distinguish color, while others perceive changes in

Horn-eyed ghost crabs' colors get darker as the sun goes down, which helps them avoid predators.

Since crabs spend much of their time in the darkness, keeping their senses alert is key to survival.

light and dark. Although crabs cannot focus clearly on objects, they can detect even the slightest movement of objects around them. When burrowing, crabs can fold their eyestalks into protective grooves against their heads. Crabs can see well in murky water and in darkness because they have a sort of night vision. But this characteristic also causes them to be temporarily blinded when flashed with a bright light in the dark.

Crabs have an acute sense of hearing, but they do not have ears. Instead, crabs rely on thousands or even millions of hairs on their body, called mechanoreceptors, to detect vibrations. The receptors then transmit the information to the crab's ganglia, a system of nerve cells throughout the body that takes the place of a brain. How quickly or slowly something vibrates is what enables a crab to "hear." For example, a big, slow wave across the water may not bother a crab, but a nearby splash would most certainly get its attention. Some hairs are sensitive to chemical signals in the air. This helps crabs locate food. The crab's two antennae (long appendages located behind the eyestalks) are covered with hairs and are especially sensitive to not only chemical signals but also touch.

The hairiest crab in the world, *Pilumnus vespertilio*, eats algae and corals and is nicknamed the teddy bear crab.

Porcelain anemone crabs use their feathery appendages like fishing nets to capture tiny passing organisms.

FEELING CRABBY

In addition to being omnivores, most crabs are detritivores, meaning they eat dead plant and animal materials.

Crabs are omnivores, meaning they can eat both animals and plants. Given a choice, they prefer to eat animals, which are more easily digested. Crabs have no teeth, so they use their claws to tear food into small bits. Three pairs of pincers called maxillipeds shove food into the mouth and down the esophagus toward the stomach. Inside the stomach, a hard structure called a gastric mill further crushes the food, while stomach juices liquefy the material for digestion. Because crabs inhabit a wide variety of environments, their diets vary greatly. Land crabs may forage for fallen fruit, while shore-dwelling crabs may survive on algae scraped from rocks. Many crabs actively hunt other animals, including smaller crabs. Nocturnal ghost crabs are a main predator of sea turtle hatchlings, and green crabs prey on clams, which they tear open with their powerful claws.

Crabs are important members of their **ecosystems** because they eat just about anything they can find, which helps keep their environments clean. Living in the **brackish** waters of mangrove forests in coastal Japan and other Pacific islands, the Sally Lightfoot crab rarely

Three species of zebra crabs are found in the Indian and Pacific oceans from Japan to Australia.

ventures onto land. This crab eats remnants of dead plants and animals as well as bodily waste dredged from the muddy floor of its habitat. Sand bubbler crabs, commonly seen on island beaches throughout the tropical Indian and Pacific oceans, burrow beneath the sand during high tide. At low tide, they emerge and begin scouring the sand for plant matter, small organisms, and carrion. They shove sand into their mouths, extract food from it, and then spit out the remaining sand in the form of balls. A colony of sand bubblers can litter a beach with thousands of balls in a matter of hours. When the tide comes back in, the crabs retreat to their burrows, and the sand balls are destroyed.

While crabs are important predators and scavengers, they also provide food for many larger animals. Dungeness crabs, weighing two to three pounds (0.9–1.4 kg), are preyed upon by large fish such as halibut and dogfish as well as wolf eels, which can weigh as much as 40 pounds (18.1 kg). Blue crabs fall prey to rays, striped bass, and even larger crabs. To escape predators, crabs typically just run away and hide, but some species have developed various defenses, including **camouflage**. Ocean-dwelling zebra crabs are able to hide from most predators by living among sea urchins. Using their stripes to blend in among the urchins, zebra crabs can hide as they harmlessly nibble on the urchins' spines.

Other methods of escaping predators require more effort on the crab's part. In a behavior called decorating, many crabs place objects on their backs to disguise themselves. The graceful kelp crab covers its body with pieces of seaweed. Tiny spines and hooks on the crab's body hold the seaweed in place. The moss crab places a living sponge on its back. When predators come near, the crab freezes, resembling nothing more than a rock and sponge. When the crab molts,

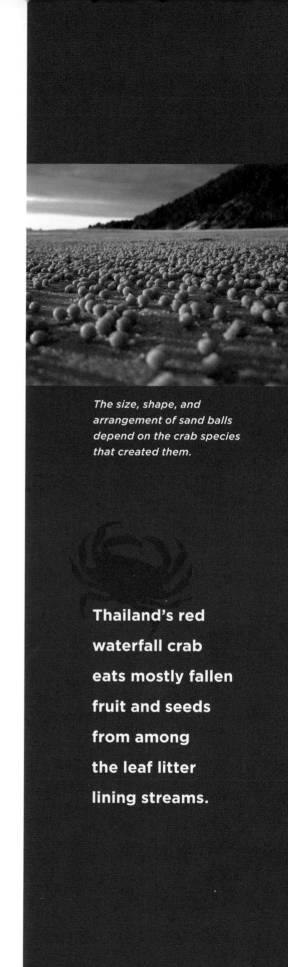

The size, shape, and arrangement of sand balls depend on the crab species that created them.

Thailand's red waterfall crab eats mostly fallen fruit and seeds from among the leaf litter lining streams.

In a behavior known as cradle carrying, a male crab carries a mating female with him to protect her.

The arrow crab (opposite) roams Caribbean coral reefs on its long, spindly legs, eating mostly bristle worms.

it takes its sponge off the old exoskeleton and puts it on the new one. Sharp-nosed and arrow crabs place a variety of creatures—tube worms, hydroids (stinging relatives of jellyfish), barnacles, and anemones—on their bodies to make themselves indistinguishable from their coral reef surroundings. Similarly, pompom crabs carry anemones in their claws. The anemones are toxic and thus not bothered by most predators. While the crabs help anemones capture more food by moving them around, the anemones provide protection for the crabs. When all else fails, a crab can avoid being eaten by purposely detaching one of its appendages— a leg or an antenna—to distract the predator long enough to escape. This is called autotomy. The appendage can then be regrown during the crab's next molt.

Young crabs unable to escape or adequately hide from predators are highly vulnerable, which is why crabs must produce thousands or even millions of offspring at a time. Mating seasons vary, depending on the crab species and their geographical locations. In general, mating occurs when the weather turns warmer. Crabs are ready to mate as soon as they reach adulthood—anytime from 12 months to 8 years old. Females mate only once in their lives,

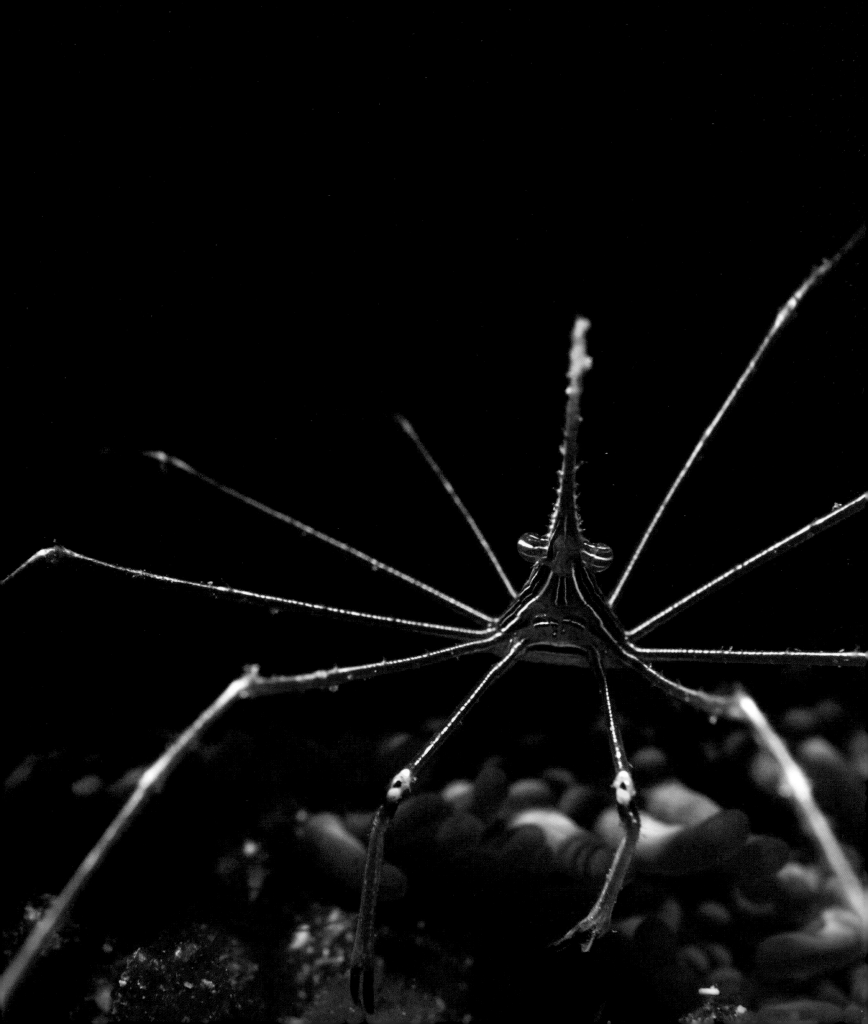

Some crab pairs may cling to each other in a pre-mating embrace lasting up to two weeks.

joining with a male in a temporary bond while molting for the last time. A male will cradle a female in his legs for a period of time, fertilizing her eggs with sperm as they leave her body. The fertilized eggs form a jellylike mass, called a sponge, which sticks to the female's apron. Some species produce several thousand eggs, while other species, such as the blue crab, may produce up to 8 million. The male remains by the female's side until her new exoskeleton hardens, protecting her as she carries her mass of eggs. When her molt is complete, the female leaves the male. The females of many species may store the males' sperm for up to two years, producing fertilized eggs several more times over the course of their lives.

All crabs, even those that live on land, must keep the developing eggs moist at all times. After one to two weeks, the female deposits the eggs in water. They immediately burst open. The hatchlings are called zoea larvae. At this point, they look nothing like their parents and are considered **zooplankton**. They have a slender tail, a needle-like projection on their back, and another projection amidst the enormous eyes on their face. The larvae go through a series of molts, drastically changing appearance each time. This process is called metamorphosis. Eventually, the sharp projections on either side of the body flatten to form the crab's round or oval body covering. The legs, claws, antennae, and eyestalks begin to develop, though the long tail is still present. This form is called a megalops. After a few more molts, the tail tightly curls against the underside, and the juvenile crab looks like a miniature version of its parents. Short-lived species, such as fiddler crabs, which live only two to three years, mature within a year. Others, such as Dungeness crabs, which can live up to 13 years, take half their lives to mature. Regardless, only one in a million zoea larvae survives to become an adult crab.

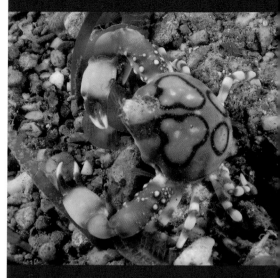

Some pebble crab species contain a poison that remains deadly to humans, even after the crab is cooked.

From Singapore to the Philippines, pebble crabs bury themselves on sandy beaches with only their carapaces showing.

The clock tower of St. Mark's Square in Venice, Italy, features the 12 zodiac symbols, including Cancer's crab.

CRABS COVER THE WORLD

D espite being the symbol for the **constellation** Cancer and 1 of the 12 signs of the zodiac (a star chart created by the ancient Babylonians), crabs are often disliked in traditional folklore. Being transformed into a crab is often a terrible curse. In a folk tale from India, an old woman loses her home and is forced to move into a tiny hut with a strange crab. After a time, the two develop great affection for each other, like a mother and son. The crab does his best to make the old woman happy, bringing her food and warm clothing. Longing for grandchildren, the old woman begs the crab to find a wife. Through a series of adventures, the crab convinces a princess to follow him home, and the young woman falls in love with the kind little crab. One day, the crab's shell is crushed in a terrible accident. The old woman and the princess cry in sorrow, and when their tears fall upon the crab, he turns into a man. Amazed, the women listen as the man explains that he was never really a crab but a prince cursed by a wicked witch.

Other crab tales are pourquoi, or stories that explain how things came to be. A legend from the Philippines

Thick-legged fiddler crabs prefer muddy mangrove habitats, where the water is rich with organic matter.

The 19th-century Japanese artist Utagawa Kuniyoshi depicted the ghost of a drowned warrior riding on the backs of crabs.

explains a common fiddler crab behavior. Long ago, the crabs became intolerant of the constant singing of the waves as they washed up on shore and then fell back into the sea. The crabs banded together to go to war with the waves in order to force them to be silent. With their heavy claws raised, the crabs raced toward the waves. But the waves were much stronger than the crabs. They crushed many of the crabs and dragged them out to sea. Some of the crabs managed to escape, but to this day, they continue to fight the waves. They rush out to chase the waves, but as soon as the waves roll onto the beach, the crabs race back to safety.

A pourquoi from Japan explains why the Heikegani crab's shell bears the likeness of a human face. At the end of the 12th century, an army known as the Heike lost a war for control of Japan. Rather than be enslaved, the Heike threw themselves into the sea, where they were transformed into the Heikegani crabs, commonly called Samurai crabs. In reality, these crabs, which are no more than two inches (5.1 cm) wide, have a muscle arrangement under their shells that just happens to resemble the face of an angry samurai warrior.

Much larger creatures are the subjects of the Discovery Channel's reality show *Deadliest Catch*, which premiered in 2005. The show's stars, **commercial** fishermen in Alaska, fish for Alaskan king crabs, which are not true crabs, for most of the year. They catch opilio (snow crabs) during the winter. More dangerous but much less publicized is the work done by fishermen who race to catch Dungeness crabs along the coast of the Pacific Northwest each fall. In 8 hours, a crew can haul in about 15,000 crabs, as long as deadly storms don't capsize their boats or throw men overboard—common threats for Dungeness crabbers. In 2007, the *Seattle Times* reported

One of the vessels featured in Deadliest Catch *is the 113-foot (34.4 m)* Time Bandit, *operated by the Hillstrand family.*

SAINT ANTHONY'S SERMON TO THE FISHES

Saint Anthony at church
Was left in the lurch,
So he went to the ditches
And preached to the fishes.
 They wriggled their tails,
 In the sun glanced their scales....

Good eels and sturgeon,
Which aldermen gorge on,
Went out of their way
To hear preaching that day.
 No sermon beside
 Had the eels so edified.

Crabs and turtles also,
Who always move low,
Made haste from the bottom
As if the devil had got 'em.
 No sermon beside
 The crabs so edified.

Fish great and fish small,
Lords, lackeys, and all,
Each looked at the preacher
Like a reasonable creature.
 At God's word,
 They Anthony heard.

The sermon now ended,
Each turned and descended;
The pikes went on stealing,
The eels went on eeling.
 Much delighted were they,
 But preferred the old way.

The crabs are backsliders,
The stock-fish thick-siders,
The carps are sharp-set,
All the sermon forget.
 Much delighted were they,
 But preferred the old way.

by Abraham a Sancta Clara
(1644–1709)

that the annual death rate of Dungeness crabbers is 50 percent higher than their Alaskan counterparts.

A crab too clever to ever get caught is Sebastian, who made his first appearance in the 1989 Disney animated film *The Little Mermaid*. As Princess Ariel's friend, Sebastian sang about life "under the sea," but the character was actually modeled after a red land crab. His musical style, called calypso, originated on the islands of Trinidad and Tobago. Sebastian appeared in two more films, *The Little Mermaid II: Return to the Sea* (2000) and *The Little Mermaid: Ariel's Beginning* (2008), as well as a television series called *Disney's The Little Mermaid* (1992–94). He also appeared in *Kingdom Hearts*, a video game series released between 2002 and 2013. His singing talent was featured on three albums: the soundtrack for *The Little Mermaid* (1989), *Sebastian from* The Little Mermaid (1990), and *Sebastian: Party Gras!* (1991).

Colorful crabs in a variety of shapes and sizes lend themselves to vibrant art, including paintings printed on postage stamps. In 2000, a set of stamps highlighted crabs found on Australia's Cocos Islands. The species featured were the horn-eyed ghost, little nipper, purple, and

Disney's The Little Mermaid *was based on the 1837 fairy tale by Danish author Hans Christian Andersen.*

Named for its black-ringed, reddish spots, the calico crab of Panama is also known as the leopard crab.

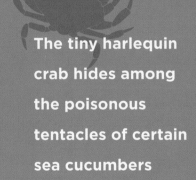

The tiny harlequin crab hides among the poisonous tentacles of certain sea cucumbers as protection from predators.

smooth-handed ghost crabs—all classified as threatened species. The Australian government donated a portion of the stamps' sales to the World Wildlife Fund. Crabs are also the subjects of a different art form: sculpture. At San Francisco's Pier 39, an enormous bronze crab with plants and flowers growing on its body welcomes visitors to the popular tourist attraction. Rising out of a pool at Vancouver's H. R. MacMillan Space Centre, a 20-foot-tall (6.1 m) stainless steel crab was never named by the artist, George Norris, who created it in 1968. It is known simply as "The Crab." In 1984, artists John and Jackie Leatherbury Douglass sculpted a 10-foot-long (3 m) and 500-pound (227 kg) Chesapeake blue crab from pieces of colored glass. The crab is part of the Baltimore/ Washington International Thurgood Marshall Airport's art collection.

Founded in 1980 as the Vero Beach Dodgers, today's Charlotte Stone Crabs are a minor-league baseball team affiliated with Major League Baseball's Tampa Bay Rays. Baseball great Cal Ripken Jr. purchased the team in 2008 and renamed it in honor of Florida's stone crab industry, which is world-renowned for its efforts in keeping

stone crab populations healthy and the crab's coastal environment safe. Much smaller than stone crabs, fiddler crabs have become a popular pet. More than 100 species of fiddler crab exist, but only some varieties are suited to life in an aquarium. Gold fiddlers are the most common. They can be kept in brackish water tanks with rocks or logs that allow the crabs time out of the water. Pet fiddlers live for about three years.

George Norris's steel crab earned the sculptor a $40,000 prize from the Canadian astronomy museum.

In 2008, paleontologists discovered a horseshoe crab fossil in Manitoba, Canada, that was nearly 450 million years old.

Crustaceans were some of Earth's first animals. The two oldest crustacean fossils ever found were chipped out of a limestone rock in England in 2001. They are about 511 million years old and only 0.02 inch (0.5 mm) wide. Using a powerful microscope, **paleontologists** were able to see the animals' body parts such as exoskeletons, antennae, and jaws. The fossilized creatures, which have yet to be named, are the ancient ancestors of modern crabs, lobsters, and other crustaceans. Crabs **evolved** about 120 million years ago and existed in virtually every ecosystem on the planet. Because Antarctica was much warmer millions of years ago, crabs were abundant there. In 1984, the first crab fossils in Antarctica were discovered. About 40 million years ago, these early crabs were mud burrowers, but as the climate cooled, they evolved into deep-sea crabs that could travel to warmer waters.

Because crab shells typically fall apart after the animal's death, only crabs whose bodies are immediately covered by mud or ash are preserved as complete fossils. Some of the best-preserved specimens have been found on Washington's Olympic Peninsula and Vancouver

Despite their name, horseshoe crabs are not crabs at all; they are more closely related to spiders.

Crab species are incredibly diverse, from devil and porcelain crabs (above) to pompom and decorator crabs (opposite).

Island in British Columbia. One species that dates to more than 25 million years ago is *Pulalius vulgaris*. This crab is an ancestor of modern crabs in the Xanthidae family, a group of more than 500 crab species known for their black-tipped claws and deadly poison.

While toxic crabs do not produce poison themselves, bacteria that live inside the crabs do—and there is no treatment for this poison. Eating particular species of Xanthid crabs will result in **paralysis** and death. The same is true of a number of other crab species, including the mosaic and shawl crabs and the devil reef crab, whose poison is so potent that one drop can kill an adult human within hours. Toxic crabs are typically brightly colored to warn away predators. Wildlife agencies in Asian countries

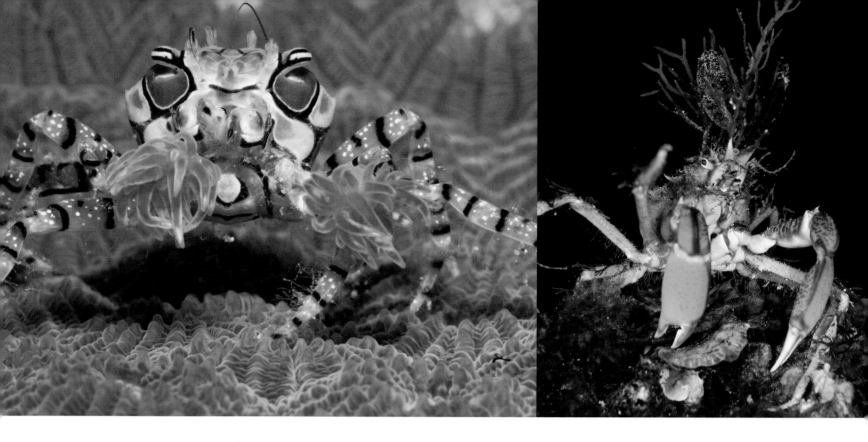

and Australia where toxic crabs exist publish guides for fishermen who may be unfamiliar with dangerous crabs.

Some crab species may pose a risk to humans, but humans have done a lot of damage to many crab populations around the world. A study coordinated by the Zoological Society of London found that freshwater crabs, which account for 20 percent of all crab species, are in trouble. Habitats of some 400 (and maybe more) of these crab species have been severely disturbed by humans. Besides destroying forests, people have also drained, diverted, and polluted water sources. The crabs affected have limited ranges in very specific habitats, mostly in tropical regions of Africa, Asia, and Australia. For example, the tree hole crab and the purple marsh

Oar-like appendages make the Sally Lightfoot crab a strong and swift swimmer as it paddles its way through water.

crab are found only in the Upper Guinean forests of Guinea and Sierra Leone in West Africa. Both are listed as endangered on the Red List of Threatened Species that is published annually by the International Union for Conservation of Nature (IUCN). Destruction of forests for agriculture presents the greatest threat to these crabs.

Because of water pollution, the critically endangered Singapore freshwater crab has disappeared from its protected area and now exists only in a single stream in the middle of a developing urban community in central

Singapore. Conservationists expect the crab to become **extinct** by 2020. More than half of the 18 members of the genus *Ceylonthelphusa*, a group of freshwater crabs found only in Sri Lanka, are also under threat. The IUCN listed three species as endangered and nine as critically endangered in 2008. Water polluted with agricultural pesticides and wetlands drained to provide more farmland are major factors in the crabs' decline. Conservationists are not hopeful for the recovery of these animals.

Scientists consider crabs a keystone species. Such animals play a vital role in maintaining the health of their ecosystems, and their absence can have devastating effects on all other organisms in the environment. Crabs are a food source for larger animals, which in turn become food for still larger predators. Crabs are also valuable predators themselves and, more importantly, essential scavengers. They clean up dead animals and plant material, and they even eat bodily waste that would otherwise pollute a habitat.

In 2010, the BP Deepwater Horizon oil spill discharged 210 million gallons (795 million l) of oil into the Gulf of Mexico, and nearly 2 million gallons (7.6

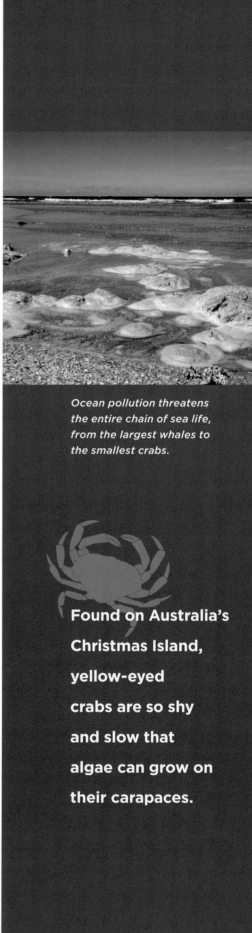

Ocean pollution threatens the entire chain of sea life, from the largest whales to the smallest crabs.

Found on Australia's Christmas Island, yellow-eyed crabs are so shy and slow that algae can grow on their carapaces.

Residents of Grand Isle, Louisiana, created a mock graveyard representing the animal deaths caused by the BP oil spill.

Soldier crabs, found in Singapore's mangrove swamps, have vents on their legs to take in oxygen when they are out of the water.

million l) of chemicals were dumped into the Gulf as part of the cleanup efforts. As one of the worst environmental disasters in recent history, the spill affected millions of animals—including crabs. Today, scientists are studying crabs to help gauge the effects of the oil spill on other animals that share the crabs' deep-sea and coastal habitats. One thing researchers have found is that crab hatchlings absorbed oil droplets, which settled under their developing exoskeletons. While most of the oil washed away when the crabs molted, any long-term damage to the crabs has yet to be analyzed. So far, fishermen and scientists working in the Gulf of Mexico have reported fish covered with sores, shrimp lacking eyes, and crabs lacking claws, among other physical deformities.

The health of many crab species is of great concern to fisheries around the world, which supply consumers with 1.5 million tons (1.4 million t) of crabs annually. Commercial crabbers are interested in only a handful of species. Japanese blue crabs, found off the coasts of East Asian countries, are the most heavily fished species, making up a quarter of the world's annual crab catch. Snow crabs are fished in the Bering Sea, brown crabs in

the North Sea, blue crabs off the eastern U.S. coast, and Dungeness crabs off the Pacific coast of North America. Flower crabs are an important species throughout Asia, and mud crabs are consumed from South Africa to Australia. While populations of commercial crab species are carefully managed, thousands of other crabs may go unnoticed, falling victim to habitat loss, pollution, and the effects of **climate change**. More attention must be given to the threatened crab species of the world so that they can continue to provide for the health of their ecosystems.

Because animals covered in sticky crude oil cannot clean themselves, they will often die without the help of humans.

ANIMAL TALE: THE CRAB AND THE MONKEY

The **cultural** history of Japan is rich with stories about animal characters that teach lessons about relationships and values. This traditional story about a selfish monkey and a generous crab illustrates the importance of sharing and the value of friendship.

Once there was an old crab who lived alone in a little cottage. Every day, she would take long walks to look for food. She would find fish heads left by fishermen and the broken rinds of *kabochas*, or Japanese pumpkins, that villagers had dropped after their meals. The old crab would always share what she scavenged, for her friends were the greatest joys in her life.

One day, as the old crab stopped to pick up six plump *ichijikus*, or figs, from the ground, she felt something hit her head. She looked up to a tree branch where a monkey

was throwing the hard pits of *momos*, or peaches, at her. "Would you like some of these figs?" she offered the monkey. "They look quite delicious."

The monkey turned up his nose. "Why do you bother sharing?" he said. "Your friends aren't real friends. They like you only because you share food with them."

"Do you have any friends?" the crab asked.

"Ha," the monkey snorted. "I could have friends if I wanted." In a flash, he scurried down the tree, snatched all the figs from the crab, and carried them back up to a high branch. Then he threw another peach pit at the crab and laughed.

The crab picked up the pits and carried them home, where she planted them in the ground beside her cottage. Every day, she poured water on the pits. Soon, one of the pits began to grow into a tiny tree. The crab

cared for the tree for several years. Then one spring day, it bloomed, and by summer, it was heavy with lovely peaches. The old crab was so happy that she planned a party and invited her friends. She wanted to share the peaches with everyone.

The night of the party, the monkey arrived before the guests and began picking the peaches, filling bags that he'd brought with him. "Remember me?" the monkey called to the crab. "That was my pit, so this is my tree, and these are my peaches."

"There are enough peaches for everyone," the crab said. "We can share."

"I think I'd rather see what happens when your so-called friends arrive and find that you have nothing to give them," the monkey said. "They will disappear in a hurry, and you'll be all alone."

When the crab's guests arrived, she explained the whole story. Everyone agreed that the tree belonged to the crab. After all, the monkey had thrown the pits at her. She had planted the pits and cared for the growing tree.

"Even so," said the crab, "if the monkey needs the tree that badly, then he should have it."

The monkey felt triumphant. He called out, "She has nothing to give you now. I will share my food with you, and you can be my friends instead."

"Go away, greedy monkey!" the crab's friends called back. "You cannot buy friendship with stolen fruit."

Ignoring the stubborn monkey, the crab and her friends sang, danced, and played games—all quite happily despite not having anything to eat.

GLOSSARY

adaptable – having the ability to change to improve one's chances of survival in an environment

appendages – parts that project from the main part of the body and have distinct functions

brackish – containing a mixture of salt water and fresh water

camouflage – the ability to hide, due to coloring or markings that blend in with a given environment

carrion – the rotting flesh of an animal

climate change – the gradual increase in Earth's temperature that causes changes in the planet's atmosphere, environments, and long-term weather conditions

commercial – used for business and to gain a profit rather than for personal reasons

constellation – a group of stars that forms a shape in the sky and has been given a name relating to that shape

cultural – of or relating to particular groups in a society that share behaviors and characteristics that are accepted as normal by that group

ecosystems – communities of organisms that live together in environments

evolved – gradually developed into a new form

extinct – having no living members

minerals – naturally occurring solid substances characterized by the formation of crystals

paleontologists – people who study fossils of animals, plants, and other organisms that existed long ago

paralysis – loss of muscle movement

parasite – an animal or plant that lives on or inside another living thing (called a host) while giving nothing back to the host; some parasites cause disease or even death

zooplankton – tiny sea creatures (some microscopic) and the eggs and larvae of larger animals

SELECTED BIBLIOGRAPHY

Chesapeake Bay Program. "Atlantic Ghost Crab." http://www.chesapeakebay.net/fieldguide/critter/atlantic _ghost_crab.

Meyer, Peter. *Nature Guide to the Carolina Coast: Common Birds, Crabs, Shells, Fish, and Other Entities of the Coastal Environment*. 2nd ed. Wilmington, N.C.: Avian-Cetacean, 2010.

National Geographic. "Animals: Blue Crab." http://animals .nationalgeographic.com/animals/invertebrates/blue-crab/.

National Geographic Education. "Red Crab Migration." http: //education.nationalgeographic.com/education/media/red -crab-migration/?ar_a=1.

Poore, Gary C. B. *Crabs, Hermit Crabs, and Allies*. Melbourne: Museum Victoria, 2007.

Washington Department of Fish & Wildlife. "Fishing and Shellfishing: Recreational Crab Fishing; Crab Identification and Biology." http://wdfw.wa.gov/fishing/shellfish/crab /identification.html.

Note: Every effort has been made to ensure that any websites listed above were active at the time of publication. However, because of the nature of the Internet, it is impossible to guarantee that these sites will remain active indefinitely or that their contents will not be altered.

When motivated, ghost crabs can race across sand at speeds approaching 10 miles (16.1 km) per hour.

INDEX